Moons, Roads, and Rivers

poems by

David J. Bauman

Finishing Line Press
Georgetown, Kentucky

Moons, Roads, and Rivers

Copyright © 2017 by David J. Bauman
ISBN 978-1-63534-369-4 First Edition
All rights reserved under International and Pan-American Copyright Conventions. No part of this book may be reproduced in any manner whatsoever without written permission from the publisher, except in the case of brief quotations embodied in critical articles and reviews.

ACKNOWLEDGMENTS

Thanks to the editors of the following publications, in which several of these poems, some in earlier versions, first appeared:

The Crucible: "Moon Watcher"
Blue Hour Magazine: "God, Dad, and Cars"
San Pedro River Review: "Elemental" and "Father"
Contemporary American Voices: "George"
Word Fountain: "For the Man in the Museum"
"Overvision," winner of the University Prize from the Academy of American Poets

Publisher: Leah Maines

Editor: Christen Kincaid

Cover Art: Michael B. McFarland

Author Photo: David McCauley

Cover Design: Elizabeth Maines McCleavy

Printed in the USA on acid-free paper.
Order online: www.finishinglinepress.com
    also available on amazon.com

Author inquiries and mail orders:
Finishing Line Press
P. O. Box 1626
Georgetown, Kentucky 40324
U. S. A.

Table of Contents

Moon Watcher 1

God, Dad, and Cars 2

Father 3

Lady Moon 4

Winter Morning Drive 5

Swim 6

Virginia Moon 9

Bubble Gum 10

In Response to Someone Who Told Me She'd
    Have to Pull Whitman Down Off the Shelf 11

Elemental 13

Road Call 14

River Art 15

George 17

Where the Bluebird Sings 19

For the Man in the Museum 20

Crossroad Song 22

Rules of Allusion 24

Overvision 27

Moon Watcher

They chuckle
softly
because once again
I have called them outside,
away from the deathly
cold light
of their television
to see the moon,
a burning globe of blood
above our street.

They nod politely.
They say, "It's lovely,"
and thank me as before.
Then my neighbors turn,
shaking their heads,
exchanging smiles,
back up the sidewalk
toward their home
and the lifeless
rays within.

God, Dad, and Cars

I'm 8 years old, perched
on a headlight under a raised hood.
Our car is white, a Chevy I think,

and it's stranded us
at Uncle Bob's farm.
But this isn't like the time

in Canada, when it broke down
along a country road, far
from home. Across the back seat

Crystal and I played cards with Mom
while you raged how God must hate
you. I wondered, why you thought

He'd bother a little family like ours,
only on vacation. Wouldn't He
have more important things to do?

No one is home at the farm,
but you know where the tools are,
your hands gloved in grease.

You are in control, under sun
and sweat. I hold something in place
while you work. Afterwards,

when the engine cranks,
you thank me, slap me on the back.
"Thank God you were here,"

you smile, as rare as your words to me,
"I couldn't have done it without you.
I couldn't have done it without you."

Father

He was born before spring, on the third day
of the third month of 1933, the year they laid
concrete on Hoover Dam. I'll never know
how he grew, slab by slab, the cold

copper veins, the gradual hardening, the dark
tunnels of blood-boiling heat and poison gas,
the tense diversion of nature's power, rushing
youth, and the life his parents built on sacrifice

and solid ground. By the time I had arrived
he was tall and solid, with a deep canyon-voice,
he kept in reserve, as behind a stone, a wall
of power, sustaining, intimidating and resolute.

Only now do I begin to know
the vast calm beauty, deep as the Mead,
that rests behind the man, and begin
to fathom what it takes to tame a wild thing.

Lady Moon

The moon goes topless tonight.
Her rise is slow; she hangs low,
uses sheer grey clouds to her advantage.
She knows she's more alluring
when she holds a little something back.

Her silver slip slides off one shoulder,
bares a shadowed breast to comets
and stars, but leaves earthmen
in longing. They wait, and hope,
but she will never show
her dark side unless they go
to her, and some have felt the pull.

The stories have it wrong, at least
by half or quarter. She's always been
a lady, moody and changing, with her push
and pull and order. She's not made
of cheese, holds no cities of flying men.
No Jackie Gleason, whistling on the wind.

Some see a man though, snared
in her negligee glow, staring ever still,
his mouth agape in surprise or song,
shock at the cold night air, celestial joy,
an orgasmic cry to last millennia, fired
by a love we wish to know,
achingly out of reach
to those of us below.

Winter Morning Drive

Crows that beat
their blue-black wings,
unhindered by the weight
of morning
    burst forth

from barren branches
onto a gray
and clouded canvas.

Envy-bound, I
stare at them
through the dusted glass,
    alone
with my reflections
of territory passed.

Swim

Age 8

Just throw him in and then he'll swim;
that was my brother's thinking,
that old adage about not sinking.
Two choices. Which would I do?

I sank. Well, first I flailed
and kicked and tried to scream,
and gulped the river in. Then I sank

and tasted it right up to my ears,
dirt and sand, and Susquehanna seaweed.
Something metal, something stone,
and something slick, the flavor
of dead or dying fish.

Like a sinker on a broken line
I was dropping fast
until he yanked me up.

On shore, minutes later,
quaking in a sandy towel—
"Hopeless," he said.
Father paddled him later
because I walked home alone.
I could still taste the river.

Age 11

In the chlorine blue of the YMCA pool
a handsome lifeguard, tanned and toned,
taught us how to tread water in the deep end.

He lived downhill from my house,
in his backyard pool had always been
kind and patient. Today there were other kids
for him to help. My arms were weak
and frantic. I sucked chemicals up my nose,

but I swear, I could taste the river.
He frowned and pulled me out,
sent me to the shallow side
where I waded with the younger kids.
When I looked back, he looked away.

Age 13

I stood on the bank, under the old
Black Bridge, my toes secretly
digging pebbled sandstone.
My friends had just transformed into fish.

We'd been splashing in the shallows.
Now their feet kicked spray.
Arms over arms, faces turning
to breathe with each stroke, they swam
through the deep water, all the way out

to the first pier. Knee-deep on its
concrete ledge they were calling to me.
I never told them what I hadn't learned.

Not far off, a train's whistle blast,
bridge metal thrumming with its approach.
Rail tie shadows riffled on the water.
I leaned forward. The sun beat down

as the coal cars thundered overhead.
I dove. Lifting my feet, arcing my back.
I remembered to turn my head and breathe

as my friends had done. Scooping my palms,
arm over arm as I had seen them do,
everything the handsome lifeguard had said
but faster, kicking with steadiness of
a ruddered fish, an instinct I didn't know I'd had.

The current was pulling me past the pier,
but I steered upriver. It was years,
it was minutes before my fingers
scraped cement and my friends tugged me up,
laughing, and splashing.

When I turned back toward the shore
it was further than I had come.
But I had done it. And I could do it again.

There was stone beneath my feet.
The river in my mouth
was metallic and sweet.

Virginia Moon

There was a little girl who cried
when the moon fell in the river.
She could not be comforted.

Grandmother's favorite—
her namesake—standing
on a kitchen chair, snow-

powdered cheeks,
up to her elbows in flour
and dough. Now

Grandmother hides ice cream
in the cupboard, runs barefoot
through the snow. She no longer

knows her granddaughter's name.
The girl has grown helpers of her own,
small fingers spreading dough.

Gingerbread men cool
in the kitchen. An angel hangs
above the door. A small boy sleeps,

his head upon her lap, an open book
against her hip, and the moon
falls to water again, finds

the window, makes white
her cheek, and glows
there in a smaller stream.

Bubble Gum

> *But the trees not carved and wall undefaced*
> *mean "Not even Kilroy was here."*
> —William Stafford, "Graffiti"

On the sheer rock wall
along Route 22 someone
has written *Bubble Gum*.

Not *Fuck You*,
or *God Hates Fags*,
not even *John 3:16*.

I've been directed by graffiti
to *Repent*, commanded
through placards to *Give*

What's Right, Not What's Left.
But now and then Kilroy
or Boone scribbles on rock

again, a message rare
as church marquees
bidding *Peace to You*.

Without telling who
was there this time,
the words merely remind—

in a flash—something good,
benign. And why complain, just
because the flavor doesn't last?

In Response to Someone Who Told Me She'd Have to Pull Whitman Down Off the Shelf.

I had simply said her lines were "Walt-ish"—
that Whitman would be happy.
There was no reason for her to get physical.

No need to pull him off the shelf.
He quietly edges out himself,
between the covers of astronomy books,
history, and politics.
He lingers a long time along the spine
of my illustrated encyclopedia of anatomy.

When my back is turned or I'm out of the house
he sometimes slips out. The mail slot maybe?

To view the people on Front Street,
or to watch stars from the roof
of our apartment building. I suspect
he slips his jacket off and suns himself

up there, bare to birds and clouds, the passing eagle
or egret soaring from one fishing spot
on the West Branch of the river

to another on the North.
He likes it here, he says, where the rivers meet,
like legs at the crotch. I often find him
strolling by the bank, below the tracks,

sometimes undisguised and naked,
a little mad. Closely peering at
a blade of grass, or watching young men
on the rowing team skiff past. Maybe
helping a small boy with a paper boat,
consoling him when it fails to float.

I once watched him tape up the ankle
of a fallen jogger, then loop his arm
under armpits as he helped her
to the bench. And once he brought
a bird home because it had a broken wing.

I find him sometimes in the morning,
between my sheets, smelling of sweat
and snoring like a river barge on cotton waves.

So quietly I lift him, slip him back
beside the other books
where he whispers in lines of love
and longing, aiding runners and riders
alike, loving the men, touching the women,

embracing—being everything, the cat, the bird,
the boat, the boy, the water's hidden current

where the river meets itself,
the broken wing,
and the eagle overhead.

Elemental

Early morning—neighbor burning trash—
flames in the barrel leap high,
mimic fire-clouds in the sky.

Fogged breath and rising smoke
disclose the face a cold, white,
waning moon. Off Middle Creek

mist exhales in longish puffs
that hover low, like frozen ghosts,
moving slower than the assembled slush

of aimless ice rafts, coasting the
current, drifting like me beneath
bare trees, not quite awake,

warming slow under a smoky moon.

Road Call

The sign said "Pass with Care"
and so I did. I cared.
I cared for the jagged,
rusty fender, the dented trunk,
the dangling tail pipe.

I cared because the bumper sticker
said, "Deadbeat Not on Board."
There were toys on the rear window ledge
and I counted three bobbing heads
with home-styled bowl cuts.

I waved from the passing lane
when I caught her eye.
Her face went white; her pale fists
clenched the steering wheel.
Eyes set straight ahead, she hit the gas.

Behind that bumper again,
alone on the wrong side of the road,
I checked my watch—
nudged the gas
and fumbled for the phone.

River Art

To my left, along the gravel road
there are only trees and campers—
pop-up, drive-up, a bare spot
for a tent, spaced every fifty feet or so,

each bordering the river,
each with an empty fire ring;
here and there a hammock,
a bird feeder, a set of wind chimes

swinging. Parallel with the road
and the river is the other shore,
all green trees from ridge-top
almost to water's edge,

along which flows
a vacant railroad track.
To my right the world ends
in high rows of feed corn

just weeks from harvest.
I have brought you with me
all this way to see them.
There, facing the river, two

women sit on yellow lawn chairs,
beyond green boughs that row the wind
the way canoeists stroke the water.
One woman wears a wide blue hat,

the other a glow-white blouse that flows
like drapes from an open window.
A child on her lap looks out from
that sill like a young queen, arms

high as if to bless her people below,
who might be the waves, or the wind,
or the trees, or the stones along the shore.
The river, moving west, seems to turn

against itself. The breeze, pushing east,
conspires with sun rays to trip
the tips of a thousand waves,
creating the illusion.

All else rests, except the hands
of the child. Fingers wiggle-reach
toward sparkles on the water.
Neither the lady in the blue hat,

nor girl in the glow-white blouse
plays a guitar, or reads a book.
No one is knitting, or talking.
And I seem to have stopped walking.

Even the birds are just
listening and watching—
the three on the bank,
and us by the road, the sun

and the waves,
and the wind at play,
the river doing one thing
and showing us another.

George

As children in the graveyard
we used to play a game
with flashlight and fear,
our minds scrambled
with a nervous delight,
a desire to be missed—
but then discovered.

Now we do like then,
but headlights pass on,
engines fade. No one waits
behind a tombstone here.

Tonight I help you home—
not far, just down the street
and across, but it takes time.
Weaving the sidewalk, we find
a stoop with three steps,
and rest a while.

No moon. No stars. No ghosts.
The other bars let out hours ago.
You and I discuss wives,
children and exes, our need
for gods, or not, thoughts
on the cross, crusades,
and inspiration, scripture
and verse, muses
and the history of prayer.

Eventually we rise,
walk wavering and slow,
not wanting you to go
as other greats have, downed
by a taxi near the tavern.

Seven more steps to the curb,
under a halo of light, you
bobbing slightly as I bring
you around. I am happy we are
here, aiming for your door,
and more than a little relieved
that the graveyard is outside of town.

Where the Bluebird Sings

I was reading from a book of essays, a letter to a mother thirty years gone.

You asked, "Did I ever tell you my dad killed a Pulitzer Prize winning author?"

The librarian arched a brow.

"It was like '93 or '95, near Santa Fe. I think he was a scientist, on his way to make a speech. In his nineties. Probably shouldn't have been driving. Pulled out right in front of Dad and—boom!

His wife wasn't hurt. And damn, if I hadn't heard about the death of this guy on NPR before mom told me—Same day Stoppard's *Arcadia* opened in London; I remember that for some reason—I was like, oh my god, my dad, the author killer!

"Hate to admit this, but it was one of me and Mom's favorite things to rib Dad about."

I put the book back and we walked outside for a smoke in the garden.
You dropped quarters in the machine and got a lemonade.
I remember birds. It was still morning, and some guy
in sandals and t-shirt was on a bench playing a guitar.

> *In memory of Wallace Stegner, Pulitzer Prize winning author of fiction who was killed as a result of injuries he obtained on April 13, 1993 when he pulled his rental car out of a side road on U.S. 184-285 into the path of my best friend's father. His last published work was in 1992, a collection of essays entitled* Where the Bluebird Sings to the Lemonade Strings.

For the Man in the Museum

> *Not in July or any month*
> *have I had the pleasure—if it is a pleasure—*
> *Of fishing on the Susquehanna.*
> —Billy Collins

Kayaking on the Susquehanna—
now that's a pleasure—in July or
any month lacking ice or floods.

I'm not sure I've ever seen a painting
of someone kayaking on the Susquehanna,
or any Pennsylvania waters for that matter.

My body feels it now, the ache that pushes
muscles as I row this rocking rhythm,
the meter of my stroke a little off—

two beats to port for each at starboard.
This fat little sit-on-top is made
for ocean waves, not upstream track.

But it's the only kayak I own, so I row
on the Susquehanna, my backyard stream.
This far north of Harrisburg where West

meets North, the water's deep, at least
when the dam is up. It's inflatable, you know,
like the egos of poets who don't know

about boats or bats that swoop past,
or fishing poles, or calloused hands,
curved paddles that dip and scoop,

and dribble Susquehanna into your lap.
It's dusk; two ducks, and a loon flap past,
wings nearly tipping the waves. I tire and drift

the way we poets do when we've pushed
the pen too hard, and need to let
the stream find us again.

The slow current spins me facing downstream,
toward a low waxing moon, and even the rise
of countless mayflies doesn't hide the glow

of pink sky above a bank of jumbled trees.
I imagine, as I glide toward shore,
a man in a museum, mind adrift,

gazing at a picture of a stranger
kayaking on the Susquehanna.
He senses something he has missed,

and thinks to write of his regret,
fleeting as a Pennsylvania rabbit,
briefly mourning a euphoria he'll never know.

Shoulders sore, a setting sun, the moon
and first few stars hover over slow
roving water. Up ahead a bass jumps

for the day's last fly. From far away I feel
his gaze. I pull my body up and out, and tug
the craft to ground, dripping the river behind me.

Crossroad Song

for Dennis

Beside the broken guard rail
someone has placed a white wooden cross
at the exact spot where a soul
made its unexpected exit out of time.

Someone grieves here and keeps this death alive,
but to those of us who motor by
it seems no more than a morbid memo,
a post-it note along the road,
a cryptic warning for us to slow it down.

Could I keep our final words alive
if I went back every Tuesday
to room 595 and sat by your empty bed,
or held the hand and kissed the head
of each new startled patient?

I would rather, if I could, visit the cabin
on Pine Creek, where summers ago
we had our talks, recall your hands
and the way you rocked

backwards when you laughed.
I'll stand by the stream
where we watched an eagle fly,
skimming its riffled surface.

And if grim disease or crunching metal
steals my life, I only ask
that my own sons not leave a plaque
in an empty room, or raise
a lonely cross along the road.

I hope instead they'll go
to Franco's on a Monday; sip
espresso, or down a beer
while they listen to the poets
read, and the music play.

And if on the road they remember me,
may it be in song, as they harmonize
again, like I once did with you,
singing alleluia, allelu.

Rules of Allusion

Swords, knives and daggers always mean
the phallus. It's about power, the myth
of control. In poetry, all literature really,
scissors are never simply about haircuts.

When writing about haircuts,
one should speak of Samson,
and the woman who stole his strength,
betrayed him to his enemies.

If composing a poem about enemies,
allude to walking in their shoes.
But be subtle. We should feel reason
for forgiveness in our souls. Think
of the hymn, "Peace Like a River."

When writing on rivers there is
no choice but to dwell on mothers,
birth waters, the ebb and flow of Time,
the source of all things,
not to mention loss, ripples,
reflections, and of course fishing.

If the poem is about fishing,
we expect a reference to the Apostle
Peter or Matthew casting nets.
Fish and fins, Huck Finn perhaps,
and the Mississippi.

Anything about Captain Ahab
and the great white whale
is gratuitous grandstanding.
Best to keep it simple, pastoral even; stick
to lost fishhooks, carelessly cast into trees.

When writing of loss, imply madness;
lost keys symbolize the loss of power
or love. But avoid that key-to-your-heart cliché,
losing ones marbles, that sort of thing.

Don't assign meaning to every tiny detail.
When you describe the barefoot boy
from a century ago, enemy of no one,
but his drunken father,
his bowl-cut hair trimmed
by a dull blade—

he would rather it be wild,
to shade his eyes from the sun
as he sets his wooden raft afloat—
he is just a boy; he is not Everyman.

He and his friend with the fishing pole
lie flat on boards, peering deep into deep.
"*Do you see them? Do you?*"

The drawstring bag lies empty between them.
Not only the marbles, but his jackknife
and a skeleton key have been lost.

No one will take you seriously,
if you say that two centuries later
you were snorkeling
in goggles and swim-fins, or believe
you spied a speck of color
on the river's stony bottom.

So how could we share in your discovery,
or watch in wonder with you
as you thumb the sand and dirt
from their surfaces and slowly
raise the relics to light?

Overvision

I wrote a poem once
about my neighbors and the moon.
Each brief line dropped
into place as I let them break
at their will. The syntax
arranged itself just comfortably
so.   Years later

I came back with more
education and a better sense
of rhythm.   I thought
I could improve
it; make the lines
more powerful,
the innuendos more profound.
                    But the new ink

was too dark for the old page,
and my good intentions discolored
the moon. I'd awakened
                a befuddled old man
and his angry, fuzzy-
slippered wife (I'd forgotten
that my old neighbors had moved
away   long ago).

They wanted to know
what the hell was going
on—who was I? And
what had I done to the sky?
Too late almost to save
it, I took whiteout
to the street (the last
bottle on the shelf
at the all-night mini
mart on that same block),

dimmed   the stars
and ushered back to bed
the little man and his grumbling
wife.   That globe of blood

        still had a pulse—
thank heaven, and I let it return
to where it had been;
on page one
of a college literary
magazine   simple
and perfect,
hanging low there
in that early night sky.

David J. Bauman was raised in the wooded hills of central Pennsylvania, but his writing first found focus while studying in the flatlands of Indiana. The poems in *Moons, Roads, and Rivers* are set against the backdrop of his return home and the challenges that followed, from reflections on his childhood to adventures in parenthood, divorce, career change, and eventually, rediscovery.

David's poems have appeared in publications like *San Pedro River Review, Contemporary American Voices, 2 Bridges Review, Barely South Review, Blue Hour, T(OUR),* and *Yellow Chair Review*. He's a winner of the Richard Savage Poetry Prize from Bloomsburg University and the Academy of American Poets.

A casual birder and avid book nerd, he now lives in northeast Pennsylvania with his partner, where he manages a small branch library and edits the literary magazine *Word Fountain*.

His second chapbook, *Angels & Adultery*, was selected by Nickole Brown for the Robin Becker Chapbook Series and is forthcoming in 2018 from Seven Kitchens Press.

www.ingramcontent.com/pod-product-compliance
Lightning Source LLC
LaVergne TN
LVHW041516070426
835507LV00012B/1617